P9-BJK-400

Cookies

Lucy Knox
and Sarah Lowman

Contents

NOTE
Standard level spoon measures are used in all recipes
Eggs should be medium unless otherwise stated
Ovens should be preheated to the specified temperature – if using a fan assisted oven, follow manufacturer's instructions for adjusting the time and the temperature.

Introduction

Making cookies is one of life's simple pleasures. Here, we show how they're tasty, fun and really quick and easy to make, because there really is nothing to compare with the flavor, texture, and quality of a proper, good old-fashioned homemade cookie.

A selection of cookies from all around the world is included, from simple drop cookies to the richest chocolate fridge squares you've ever tasted, and most of them take no more than half an hour to make.

The history

Cookies or biscuits? In Great Britain, the words are used as if they were synonymous but, to be strict in both a linguistic and culinary sense, they're not. Biscuit means cooked twice. The word comes from the French *bescoit* and reflects how the first biscuits were made. These were small, flat, round cakes made of wheat flour, sugar, egg yolks, and sometimes yeast. They were intended for long keeping, so were baked twice, to insure they would stay dry and crisp for some time. The addition of yeast to the dough led to them being known as biscuit bread. The dough would be shaped into rolls, then sliced and baked, and the result was a biscuit similar to a rusk. Sailors took these biscuits to sea, since they kept well during a long voyage.

of cookies

In the United States, it is a different story. We call the British biscuit a cookie, and only savory crackers are sometimes called biscuits. The word "cookie" was introduced to North America in the late eighteenth century by Dutch settlers. It comes from the Dutch word *koekje*, which means cake.

The first cookies were created in Europe in the seventeenth century. They were a kind of honey cake—honey being the only sweetener then available—and although the dough itself was very simple, these early cookies were often elaborately decorated. They were made as a special treat, baked in intricate molds and exquisitely iced. The German gingerbread house is probably the best-known example.

The modern store-bought cookie is essentially the product of nineteenth century industrialization and twentieth century promotion and packaging. Cookies have grown into a very big business.

Spices

It's amazing the difference a touch of spice makes. Once you've found a favorite cookie recipe, try adding some ground spice and you'll be amazed at the results. There's nothing to beat a gingersnap, and the recipe here is made spicier by using ginger stems in syrup as well as ground ginger. You can try the more unusual spices too, such as ground cardamom, which gives the pretty cardamom and orange cookies a really delicious fragrant flavor.

The Shrewsbury cookie can be spiced up with cinnamon and nutmeg for those who like a more robust flavor. And the brandy snaps can be made really spicy by doubling the quantity of allspice.

Other spices to experiment with are ground cinnamon, ground nutmeg, ground star anise, and ground cumin.

Shaping cookies

Don't feel you have to stick rigidly to the shapes and molds used in these recipes; there is a wide range of new shapes in the stores today. Obviously it's useful to have a set of fluted or round cookie cutters but look out for stars, crescent moons, and hearts. For children, there are animal shapes and gingerbread people molds, and for Christmas, stocking and tree-shaped molds.

Tuiles and brandy snaps are simple cookies, made by the melting method, which can be molded while warm into any number of sophisticated shapes. Try shaping brandy snaps over an orange to make fluted baskets or forming tuiles around metal cones, ready to fill with strawberries and cream.

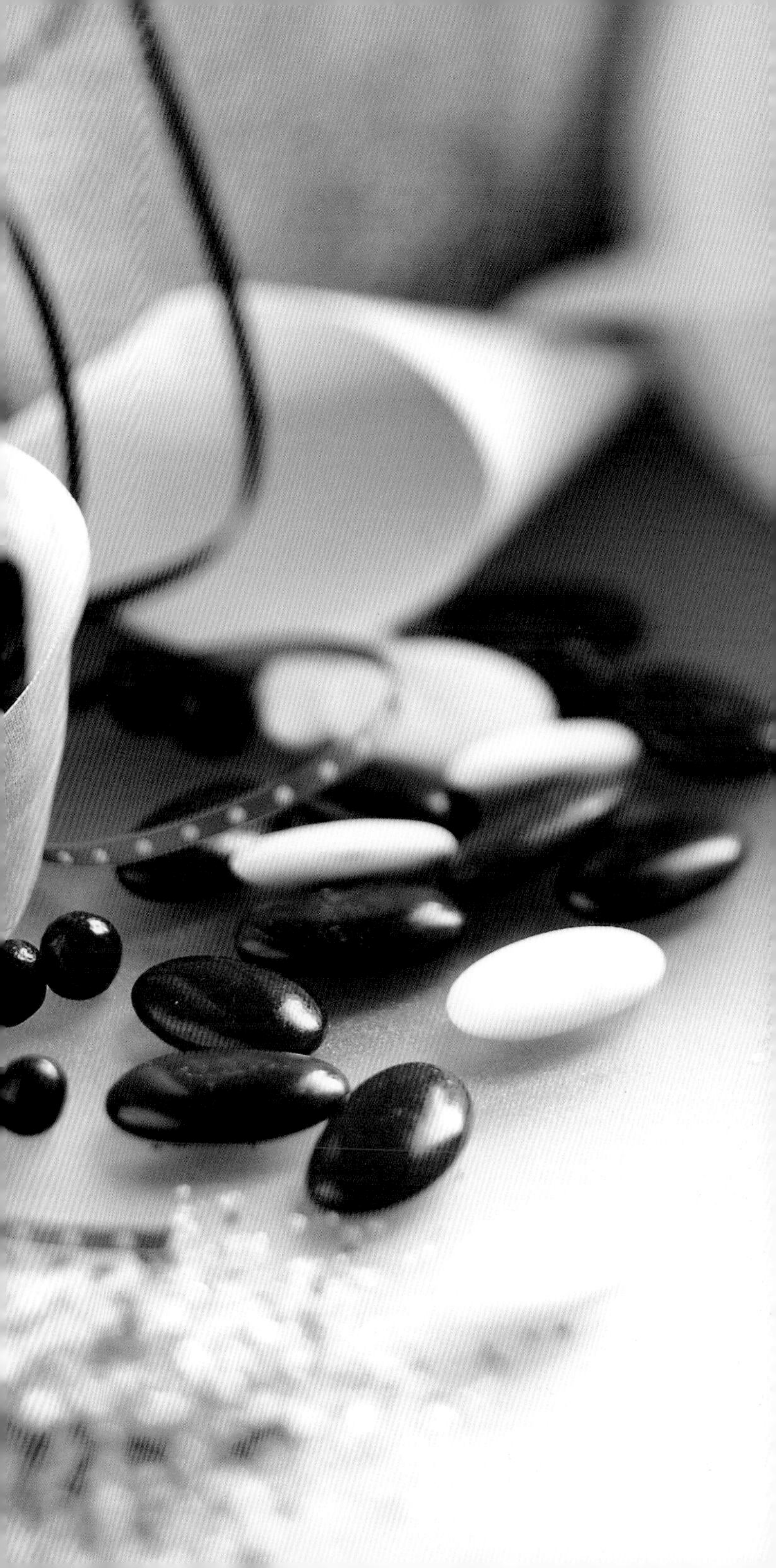

Decorating cookies

The days of intricate, iced cookies are long past. The modern way of decorating cookies is to simply dust them with confectioners' sugar. Put a sheet of waxed paper over part of the cookie and then dust the uncovered part with the sifted sugar. The effect is stunning. To add extra flavor, try adding a pinch of allspice or cocoa powder to the confectioners' sugar.

If you really enjoy decorating cookies, the best frosting to use is glacé icing. There's no need to measure out the confectioners' sugar, just tip a couple of tablespoonfuls into a bowl and then add enough cold water—you'll only need a few drops—to make a smooth piping consistency. For extra flavor, substitute lemon or orange juice for the water. In this book, glacé icing is used to decorate the Christmas cookies, but you could, of course, brush the cookies with a little clear honey and top them with chopped nuts, or candied fruits, to make simple but effective decorations.

Perhaps the most attractive and mouth-watering form of decoration is simply to dip the cookie in a little melted chocolate. When you do this, it looks more effective when you coat either one side or one half of the cookie, rather than completely covering the whole cookie.

If the cookies are to be a gift, stack them in portion-sized piles and tie them up with a pretty ribbon. This takes no time at all and the effect is magnificent.

Rituals

Most homes nowadays have a jar of cookies in the kitchen, ready to enjoy with a cup of coffee. The most famous American cookie, the chocolate chip, was created in 1935 by Ruth Wakefield in Massachusetts. The other all-American bar cookie is, of course, the irresistible brownie. Across the Atlantic they have their own proud traditions. The most famous British indigenous cookie is shortbread, but other favorites include the Shrewsbury cookie, the jammy dodger, and the brandy snap.

Cookies are a great favorite all over Europe. In the seventeenth and eighteenth centuries a kind of cookie madness used to descend on central Europe during December. Women would bake batch upon batch of cookies for their families to exchange on Christmas Day, a tradition that persists to this day and explains the proud baking heritage of spritz, sablés, and chocolate pretzels in Austria, Germany, and Switzerland.

In Scandinavia, too, there is a fine tradition of cookie making, including the famous "S" cookies from Finland, cherry half-moons from Sweden, and a range of deliciously delicate iced cookies, made in Denmark.

Eastern Europe produces rather more robust cookies, such as the honey and almond cookie from Poland and the poppy seed cookie from Bulgaria.

In southern Europe, around the Mediterranean, there is a tradition of baking rich, colorful cookies. Italy, in particular, has a long history of cookie making, often using an abundance of nuts, fresh citrus and candied fruits, and producing treats like *biscotti* and iced cookies. The French really enjoy cookies made with chocolate, while the Spanish and Portuguese prefer meringue-style cookies.

and customs

Triple chocolate

½ cup butter
⅓ cup soft light brown sugar
⅓ cup sugar
1 egg
1½ cups self-rising flour
2 oz semisweet chocolate, coarsely chopped
2 oz white chocolate, coarsely chopped
2 oz milk chocolate, coarsely chopped

1 Lightly grease two cookie sheets. Beat the butter with the two sugars. Beat in the egg, sift the flour over the mixture and stir in with all the chopped chocolate.

2 Using a teaspoon, drop teaspoonfuls of the mixture, well apart, on to the cookie sheets. Bake in a preheated oven at 375°F, for 12 minutes, or until golden brown.

3 Let cool for 1 minute, then transfer to a wire rack to cool.

Makes about 32
Preparation time: 15 minutes
Cooking time: 12 minutes

Chunky chocolate nut

½ cup butter, softened
¾ cup soft brown sugar
1 egg, lightly beaten
1¼ cups all-purpose flour
½ teaspoon baking powder
1 cup oats
7 oz semisweet chocolate, coarsely chopped
½ cup almonds, coarsely chopped
confectioners' sugar or unsweetened cocoa powder, for dusting

1 Grease two cookie sheets. Beat the butter and sugar until creamy. Add the egg, flour, baking powder, and oats and beat until mixed. Stir in the chocolate and almonds.

2 Put dessertspoonfuls, spaced slightly apart, on the cookie sheets. Flatten gently with a fork and bake in a preheated oven at 350°F, for 15–20 minutes until firm and pale golden in color.

3 Leave on the cookie sheets for 2 minutes, then transfer to a wire rack to cool. Serve dusted with confectioners' sugar or cocoa powder.

Makes about 28
Preparation time: 15 minutes
Cooking time: 15–20 minutes

Chocolate chip

½ cup butter, softened
⅓ cup soft brown sugar
1 egg, beaten
½ teaspoon vanilla extract
1½ cups self-rising flour
½ teaspoon baking powder
6 oz semisweet chocolate, chopped

1 Grease two cookie sheets. Beat the butter with the sugar until light and fluffy. Add the egg and vanilla extract and beat well. Sift the flour and baking powder and stir in with the chocolate to make a stiff dough.

2 Using a dessertspoon, place spoonfuls, spaced slightly apart, on the cookie sheets and bake in a preheated oven at 350°F, for 15–18 minutes.

3 Leave the cookies on the cookie sheets for 2 minutes, then transfer to a wire rack to cool.

Makes about 20
Preparation time: 15 minutes
Cooking time: 15–18 minutes

Peanut butter and raisin

¾ cup peanut butter
½ cup butter
½ cup sugar
⅓ cup soft brown sugar
½ teaspoon vanilla extract
1 egg, beaten
1¼ cups all-purpose flour
½ teaspoon baking powder
¾ teaspoon baking soda
¼ teaspoon salt
3 tablespoons raisins, chopped

1 Grease two cookie sheets. Cream the peanut butter, butter, and both sugars. Beat in the vanilla and egg. Sift the flour, baking powder, baking soda, and salt. Beat into the peanut mixture with the raisins and mix to a soft dough. Chill for 30 minutes.

2 Roll the dough into walnut-sized balls and place well apart on the cookie sheets. Dip a fork in flour and lightly flatten the cookies in a crisscross pattern. Bake in a preheated oven at 375°F, for 10–12 minutes. Leave on the cookie sheets for 1 minute, then transfer to a wire rack to cool.

Makes about 35

Preparation time: 15 minutes, plus chilling

Cooking time: 10–12 minutes

Tollhouse cookies

½ cup butter
3 tablespoons soft brown sugar
½ cup sugar
1 egg, beaten
1 teaspoon vanilla extract
1¼ cups all-purpose flour
¼ teaspoon baking soda
½ teaspoon salt
4 oz semisweet chocolate, coarsely chopped

1 Grease two cookie sheets. Beat the butter with both sugars until light and fluffy. Add the egg and vanilla extract, and mix well. Sift together the flour, baking soda, and salt. Stir in the sifted dry ingredients and chocolate.

2 Place teaspoonfuls of the mixture, spaced apart, on the cookie sheets and bake in a preheated oven at 350°F, for 10 minutes. Transfer to a wire rack to cool.

Makes about 36

Preparation time: 10 minutes

Cooking time 10 minutes

Shrewsbury cookies

¼ cup butter, softened
¼ cup sugar
1 egg
1½ cups all-purpose flour
½ teaspoon allspice
⅓ cup currants, washed and dried
1 tablespoon sugar, for sprinkling

1 Grease two cookie sheets. Beat the butter with the sugar until pale and fluffy. Beat in the egg. Sift the flour and allspice over the mixture and fold in with the currants. Knead the dough lightly.

2 Roll out the dough on a lightly floured surface. Using a 3-inch fluted cutter, cut it into cookies. Transfer to the cookie sheets and bake in a preheated oven at 375°F, for 5 minutes.

3 Sprinkle with sugar and return to the oven for a further 10 minutes, or until cookies are lightly browned.

4 Leave the cookies on the cookie sheets for 1 minute, then transfer to a wire rack to cool.

Makes about 16
Preparation time: 15 minutes
Cooking time: 15 minutes

Oat and raisin

½ cup raisins
½ cup hot water
¾ cup butter
¾ cup soft brown sugar
1 egg, beaten
1 teaspoon vanilla extract
1 cup all-purpose flour
1 teaspoon salt
½ teaspoon baking soda
½ teaspoon ground cinnamon
2½ cups oats

1 Cover the raisins with the hot water and let stand for 15 minutes. Drain well and reserve ¼ cup of the water.

2 Beat the butter and sugar until pale and creamy. Stir in the egg, vanilla, and raisins. Sift the flour, salt, baking soda, and cinnamon over the mixture. Stir well, adding the reserved water and oats, to make a soft dough.

3 Using a dessertspoon, place spoonfuls, well apart, on greased cookie sheets. Flatten slightly with a fork. Bake in a preheated oven at 375°F, for 15–20 minutes.

4 Leave on the sheets for 2 minutes, then transfer to a wire rack to cool.

Makes about 25
Preparation time: 15 minutes
Cooking time: 15–20 minutes

Walnut cookies

1 cup butter
1⅓ cups confectioners' sugar, sifted
1 egg, beaten
1 teaspoon vanilla extract
2¾ cups all-purpose flour
½ teaspoon baking soda
1 teaspoon baking powder
¼ teaspoon salt
1½ cups walnuts, finely chopped
about 36 walnut halves, to decorate

1 Lightly grease two cookie sheets. Beat the butter with the confectioners' sugar. Add the egg and vanilla extract and beat well. Sift the flour with the baking soda, baking powder, and salt. Stir into the mixture with the chopped nuts.

2 Form the mixture into small balls, the size of walnuts, place on the cookie sheets and top each one with a walnut half. Bake in a preheated oven at 375°F, for 10–12 minutes, or until lightly browned. Transfer to wire racks to cool.

Makes about 36
Preparation time: 15 minutes
Cooking time: 10–12 minutes

Hazelnut cookies

1¼ cups self-rising flour
6 tablespoons sugar
¾ cup toasted hazelnuts, coarsely chopped
⅔ cup butter

1 Grease two cookie sheets. Sift the flour into a bowl and stir in the sugar and hazelnuts. Rub in the butter until the mixture resembles coarse crumbs. Work the mixture to a dough.

2 Pinch pieces of dough, the size of walnuts, and roll into balls. Place on the cookie sheets and flatten lightly with a fork.

3 Bake the cookies in a preheated oven at 350°F, for 10–12 minutes, or until golden brown. Leave the cookies on the cookie sheets for about 1 minute, then transfer to a wire rack to cool.

Variation

Pecan cookies

Toast and coarsely chop 1 cup pecans and substitute them for the hazelnuts, and use vanilla sugar in place of the regular sugar.

Makes about 30

Preparation time: 15 minutes

Cooking time: 10–12 minutes

Gingersnaps

1 cup self-rising flour
½ teaspoon baking soda
2 teaspoons ground ginger
1 tablespoon sugar
¼ cup butter
¼ cup light corn syrup
1 tablespoon chopped ginger stems in syrup, drained
about 24 slivered almonds

1 Grease two cookie sheets. Sift the flour, baking soda, ground ginger, and sugar. Melt the butter with the corn syrup and then stir into the sifted mixture with the chopped ginger.

2 With wet hands, break off walnut-sized pieces of cookie dough and roll into balls. Place the balls slightly apart on the cookie sheets and flatten gently with a palette knife. Arrange a slivered almond on top of each ball.

3 Bake the cookies in a preheated oven at 400°F, for 8–10 minutes. Leave to cool slightly on the cookie sheets, then transfer to a wire rack to cool.

Makes about 24
Preparation time: 20 minutes
Cooking time: 8–10 minutes

Cardamom and orange

½ cup butter, softened
⅔ cup sugar
1 egg, beaten
2¼ cups all-purpose flour
1 tablespoon green cardamom pods, pods removed and seeds ground

ORANGE CREAM

¼ cup butter, softened
¾ cup confectioners' sugar, sifted
grated rind of 1 orange

1 Grease two cookie sheets. Beat the butter and sugar until creamy. Beat in the egg. Sift the flour over and stir in with the cardamom. Knead lightly, then shape into a roll about 2-inches in diameter. Chill for 1 hour.

2 Cut the roll into ½-inch slices and arrange slightly apart on the cookie sheets. Bake in a preheated oven at 375°F, for 10 minutes. Leave on the cookie sheets for 2 minutes, then cool on a wire rack.

3 Make the orange cream: beat the butter and confectioners' sugar until smooth. Stir in the rind. Use to sandwich the cookies together.

Makes about 18

Preparation time: 25 minutes, plus chilling

Cooking time: 10 minutes

Lemon and pistachio

1 cup butter
¾ cup confectioners' sugar, sifted
3 cups all-purpose flour
1 egg yolk
grated rind of 1 lemon
½ cup pistachio nuts, chopped
green food coloring

1 Grease two cookie sheets. Beat the butter and sugar until pale and creamy. Fold in the flour and egg yolk. Mix to form a firm dough.

2 Divide the dough in half and stir the lemon rind into one half and the nuts and green food coloring into the other. Cover both mixtures and chill for about 2 hours.

3 Roll each piece of dough into a 9 x 6-inch rectangle and place one on top of the other. Roll gently once, then roll up, jelly-roll style. Cover and chill for 30 minutes.

4 Cut the roll into about 35 slices and arrange on the cookie sheets. Bake in a preheated oven at 350°F, for 15–16 minutes, or until golden. Cool on a wire rack.

Makes 35
Preparation time: 20 minutes, plus chilling
Cooking time: 15–16 minutes

Spiced Christmas cookies

½ cup butter
⅓ cup soft brown sugar
1¼ cups all-purpose flour
1 teaspoon ground cinnamon
¼ teaspoon ground cloves
¼ teaspoon ground nutmeg
¼ teaspoon ground ginger
1 egg, beaten

1 Grease two cookie sheets. Beat the butter and sugar until fluffy. Sift the flour, cinnamon, cloves, nutmeg, and ginger over the butter mixture, and fold in gently. Stir in the beaten egg and mix to a firm dough. Knead lightly. Wrap and chill for 4 hours.

2 Roll out the mixture to ¼-inch thick on a lightly floured surface. Dip your chosen cookie cutters into a little flour to prevent them sticking and cut the dough into shapes.

3 Arrange the cookies on the cookie sheets and bake in a preheated oven at 350°F, for 10–12 minutes. Leave on the cookie sheets for 1 minute to firm, then cool on a wire rack.

Makes about 24

Preparation time: 25 minutes, plus chilling

Cooking time: 10–12 minutes

Variation

Gingerbread people

Omit the ground cinnamon, cloves, and nutmeg. Increase the ground ginger to 1 teaspoon and cut out about 6 gingerbread people. Bake as for the main recipe.

Makes about 6

Preparation time: 25 minutes, plus chilling

Cooking time: 10–12 minutes

Christmas cookies

6 tablespoons butter, softened
½ cup sugar
1 egg, plus 1 egg yolk
1½ cups all-purpose flour, sifted
TO DECORATE
glacé icing (see page 18)
colored sugar balls
colored sugared almonds, chopped

1 Beat the butter and sugar until pale and creamy. Mix in the eggs and then gradually add the flour. Knead lightly and roll out on a lightly floured surface to a ½-inch thickness. Cut out shapes using floured cookie cutters. To hang them on the Christmas tree, make a small hole near one end with a skewer.

2 Transfer the cookies to a cookie sheet and bake in a preheated oven at 350°F, for 15–20 minutes, until golden brown.

3 Leave the cookies on the cookie sheet for 1 minute, then cool on a wire rack.

4 To decorate the cookies, dip them into the glacé icing, then sprinkle them with the sugar balls and chopped almonds.

Makes about 24

Preparation time: 25 minutes

Cooking time: 15–20 minutes

Rock cookies

¼ cup boiling water
¾ cup raisins
¼ cup butter, softened
¾ cup soft brown sugar
1 egg
¼ cup walnuts or hazelnuts, finely chopped
1¼ cups all-purpose flour
½ teaspoon baking powder
½ teaspoon salt
½ teaspoon ground cinnamon

1 Grease two cookie sheets. Pour the boiling water over the raisins and set aside.
2 Beat together the butter and sugar until light and fluffy. Beat in the egg. Stir in the nuts. Sift together the flour, baking powder, salt, and cinnamon. Stir the dry ingredients into the creamed mixture with the raisins and their liquid. Beat the mixture well.
3 Place heaped teaspoonfuls of the mixture on the cookie sheets, spaced well apart, and bake in a preheated oven at 350°F, for 15–20 minutes.
4 Leave the cookies on the cookie sheets for 1 minute to firm, then cool on a wire rack.
Makes about 20
Preparation time: 10 minutes
Cooking time: 15–20 minutes

Swirl cookies

1 cup butter, softened
¼ cup sugar
1 tablespoon lemon juice
grated rind of 1 lemon
2¼ cups all-purpose flour, sifted
TO DECORATE
chocolate covered coffee beans
candied cherries, chopped
colored sugar

1 Beat the butter and sugar until light and fluffy. Stir in the lemon juice and rind. Fold in the flour and stir until the mixture is smooth. Spoon the mixture into a pastry bag, fitted with a star nozzle, and pipe about 30 swirls into mini paper cases.

2 Decorate the cookies with chocolate covered coffee beans, candied cherries, or colored sugar. Chill for about 30 minutes.

3 Bake the cookies in a preheated oven at 350°F, for 15–18 minutes. Leave on the cookie sheets for 1 minute, then transfer to a wire rack to cool.

Makes about 30
Preparation time: 20 minutes, plus chilling
Cooking time: 15–18 minutes

Boston brownies

1 cup butter, softened
1 cup soft brown sugar
4 eggs, beaten
1 teaspoon vanilla extract
2 cups all-purpose flour
1 teaspoon baking powder
½ teaspoon salt
½ cup unsweetened cocoa powder
1 cup toasted hazelnuts, chopped
4 oz semisweet chocolate, chopped
4 oz mini marshmallows

1 Grease and line the base of a 12 x 8 x 2-inch cake pan.

2 Beat the butter with the soft brown sugar until light. Gradually beat in the eggs and vanilla. Sift the flour, baking powder, salt, and cocoa powder over the batter and fold in. Stir in the hazelnuts, chocolate, and mini marshmallows.

3 Spoon the batter into the prepared pan and bake in a preheated oven at 350°F, for 30–35 minutes. Leave in the pan to cool, before cutting into 12 pieces.

Makes about 12
Preparation time: 15 minutes
Cooking time: 30–35 minutes

Millionaire's shortbread

BASE

1 cup butter

½ cup soft brown sugar

3 cups all-purpose flour, sifted

FILLING

1 cup butter

½ cup sugar

1¾ cups canned evaporated milk

4 tablespoons clear honey

TOPPING

8 oz semisweet chocolate, coarsely chopped

2 tablespoons butter

2 oz white chocolate, coarsely chopped

1 To make the base, first grease a 12 x 8 x 2-inch cake pan. Beat the butter and sugar until pale and creamy, then stir in the flour to form a smooth dough. Knead lightly before pressing into the pan. Prick the base evenly with a fork. Bake in a preheated oven at 350°F, for 45 minutes. Leave to cool in the pan.

2 Put all the ingredients for the filling into a saucepan. Heat slowly, until the butter has melted and the sugar dissolved, stirring occasionally. Bring to the boil, then simmer for 3–5 minutes, or until the mixture is golden, stirring all the time. Pour the filling over the cooled base and leave it to set.

3 To make the topping, melt the semisweet chocolate and butter in a bowl set over a pan of simmering water. Melt the white chocolate separately in the same way. Pour the semisweet chocolate over the filling and leave to set for 2 minutes before dotting with the melted white chocolate. Using a skewer, drag the white chocolate through the semisweet to make a pattern. Leave to set before cutting into bars.

Makes about 33

Preparation time: 20 minutes

Cooking time: 55 minutes

Brandy snaps

¼ cup butter
¼ cup sugar
2 tablespoons light corn syrup
½ cup all-purpose flour
½ teaspoon allspice
1 teaspoon brandy

1 Line two cookie sheets with nonstick waxed paper. Melt the butter, sugar, and light corn syrup over a gentle heat, stirring occasionally. Stir, off the heat, until smooth. Sift the flour and allspice over the mixture, then add the brandy and beat until smooth.

2 Using a teaspoon, place a few spoonfuls of the mixture, spaced apart, on the cookie sheets and bake in batches in a preheated oven at 350°F, for 7–10 minutes.

3 Leave the brandy snaps on the cookie sheets for 1 minute, then lift off the sheets with a palette knife. Wrap the brandy snaps around the handles of greased wooden spoons and leave until set before sliding off and leaving to cool completely on a wire rack. Repeat with the remaining mixture.

Makes about 25
Preparation time: 20 minutes
Cooking time: 7–10 minutes per batch

Chocolate fridge cookies

1 cup butter
½ cup confectioners' sugar
3 tablespoons light corn syrup
4 tablespoons unsweetened cocoa powder
½ cup candied orange, chopped
½ cup candied ginger, chopped
12 oz graham crackers, crushed
8 oz semisweet chocolate, chopped, to decorate

1 Grease and line the base of a 12 x 8 x 1½-inch cake pan.

2 Put the butter, confectioners' sugar, light corn syrup, and cocoa powder into a saucepan and heat gently until the butter has melted, stirring occasionally. Combine the chopped orange and ginger with the crushed crackers and pour over the melted mixture. Stir well. Spoon the mixture into the prepared cake pan and smooth level with the back of a spoon. Cover and chill for at least 1 hour.

3 Melt the semisweet chocolate and pour over the base. Leave to set before cutting into bars.

Makes 24 bars

Preparation time: 10 minutes, plus chilling

Coffee kisses

3 egg whites

¾ cup sugar

1 tablespoon instant coffee powder

⅔ cup heavy cream, lightly beaten

1 Line two cookie sheets with waxed paper. Beat the egg whites until stiff. Gradually beat in the sugar with the coffee. Spoon into a pastry bag, fitted with a star nozzle, and pipe 40 small swirls on the cookie sheets.

2 Bake in a preheated oven at 225°F, for 2–2½ hours, or until the meringues are crisp and dry.

3 Set aside the meringues to cool before sandwiching together with the cream.

Makes 20

Preparation time: 15 minutes

Cooking time: 2–2½ hours

Tuiles

2 egg whites
¼ cup vanilla sugar
½ cup all-purpose flour
¼ cup butter or margarine, melted

1 Line a cookie sheet with nonstick waxed paper. Lightly beat the egg whites and stir in the vanilla sugar. Sift the flour over the mixture and stir together gently. Fold in the melted butter or margarine.

2 Using a teaspoon, drop spoonfuls of the mixture on to the cookie sheet. With the back of the spoon, smooth the mixture into 3-inch rounds and bake in a preheated oven at 400°F, for 5–7 minutes, or until pale golden brown around the edges.

3 Remove at once from the cookie sheet with a palette knife and shape around a rolling pin to make tuiles. Alternatively, use metal cornet molds to make cornets, or the handles of wooden spoons to make "cigarette" cookies. Leave to cool.

Makes about 18
Preparation time: 20 minutes
Cooking time: 5–7 minutes per batch

Index

First published in the UK in 1996 by Hamlyn
an imprint of Reed International Books Limited

Printed in China

Photography by Peter Myers